What Others Are Saying

THE MIDWEST BOOK REVIEW

". . . Every novel, regardless of its genre, needs to open with a hook, and then irresistibly propel the reader to dive in and become immersed in the story from beginning to end. ROBIN by Kenneth Shelby Armstrong is just such a novel and highly recommended as an original and carefully crafted story from first page to last."

James A. Cox, Editor-in-Chief

Marilyn A. Hudson

Armstrong's "Robin" Soars High.

"Oklahoma author Kenneth Shelby Armstrong presents a story of lyrical beauty, deeply felt emotion, thought provoking actions, and lasting inspiration."

Marilyn A. Hudson Reviewer

"An interesting, even compelling collection. Some of the essays have phrases that have that lasting impact worth repeating, rising to the level of superb writing."

T. W. Jones, attorney at Law
Colorado Springs, Colorado

"Armstrong shows unusual insight into his subject and has the literary skill to express it forcefully and meaningfully."

Val J. Christensen, Ph.D.
Educator, San Diego, California

"I read your book in one sitting. It is truly a fine piece of work. Your writing is superb."

James D. Hamilton,Ed.D.
Psychologist,
Austin, Colorado

"Great project! I've never seen a similar one."

Forrest Ladd, Ph.D.
University Vice President

"The wit, wisdom and wealth of words that powerfully communicate from your soul to ours, is a gift and anointing I've known of you for 55 years. Keep it up."

Walter Thomas, Ed.D.
Educator, Speaker, Motivater

"Fascinating experience, and one that I did not know you had! Indeed your life seems to unfold into a story book of rich adventures, each a puzzle piece in a most dynamic, influential and inspirational life!"

Vivian Stewart
Poet, Author, Artist, Creator

I have so enjoyed reading these four books by a local, very intelligent, gifted writer in our community...Dr. Kenneth Armstrong...I would encourage you all to partake in his history by purchasing them on Amazon.. his stories are amazing.

Sean Boone, D.O.
Hugo, Oklahoma

Win With Wisdom

Series

ksa

Kenneth Shelby Armstrong Th.D., Ed.D.

Copyright © 2017

"WISDOM in Knowing Yourself and Others"

Why You And Others Do What They Do

Kenneth Shelby Armstrong Th.D., Ed.D.

"WISDOM in Knowing Yourself and Others"

Why You And Others Do What They Do

Psychology has become one of the most popular studies in colleges and universities. Unfortunately it has been seized by the academicians who have morphed it into a complex tool, available only to the esoteric.

This book attempts to mold psychology into a useful every-day tool for average persons. There are no long words or complex formulas. The average person can use what he reads to understand himself and those with whom he lives and works.

That it is a common sense book for daily living is its merit, but don't show it to your professor, analyst or therapist. Read it yourself and use it daily.

During our life-times the most common answer to why people do what they do has been called the stimulus-response (S/R) solution. Another way of explaining this answer is called BEHAVIORISM.

BEHAVIORISM is a systematic approach that assumes that all behavior is either reflex produced by a response to certain stimuli in the environment, or a consequence of that individual's history, including a controlling stimulus. Now, if that definition doesn't grab you, try this one.

BEHAVIORISM is the study of cause and effect in human relationships. Something happens to the human being and that *causes* a particular response or effect to that event. In common language we often hear these kind of expessions:

"I wonder what's eating him."

"What made her do a fool thing like that?"

"No matter what I try, I can't get him to keep his room clean."

"I thought a weekly allowance would make her a little more responsible with her chores."

"I've tried everything and still he refuses to do his homework."

The Behaviorist (and most politicians) believe that if you can influence a person in just the right way, you can cause them to do almost anything that you want them to do.

I call this the **billiard** approach. All those balls are on the table and they are not moving. Now if I hit that ball on the left side it will make the ball go to the right and into the cup. The guy who knows how the ball will react if he hits the right spot, will win the game.

Thus, all of us spend too much of our lives trying to find that sweet spot that makes others do what you want them to do.

"Try flattery. That usually works with most people."

"Try threatening people with dire consequences if they don't do what you ask them to do."

"Try reward. Promise them something good if they will only act the way you desire"

"Try Fear. Fear is a great motivator so show them what is just around the corner if they don't shape up."

Use **words** to cause behavioral response:

"He is a **social democrat**, or he is a **communist**." The difference between those two words is close, but the behavioral response to each is miles apart.

"She has had a very favorable up-bringing. Or She is a spoiled brat." The emotional difference between these two descriptions is large, and we have used this knowledge to try to make people do what we want them to do.

The big problem with BEHAVIORISM is not that it is false, but that it is only *partially* true. No matter how adept you become in using stimulus/response, it will not always work. Flattery does not always work. Threat does not always work.

With some people, at certain times, you can threaten them with **death** and still they will refuse to act the way you want them to act. No matter how hard you try to master your *stimulus techniques*, they will simply let you down at very important times.

We have finally learned (some have learned) that the human being can be self actualizing. That is, the human being has the capacity to act without any outside stimulus. Mankind can be self-activating and impervious to your best stimulative efforts.

If stimulus doesn't work, what will work? Perhaps we need a new theory of what makes human behavior perform like it does. Let's try a new approach. It's called perceptional psychology, and it is based on several axioms.

BEHAVIOR is a
function of Perception.

The human being always acts in a way that is consistent with how he **sees or perceives** himself or the event. This theory says that behavior is the result of how things **seem** to the perceiver. Perceptions lie inside the person. The secret is that behavior comes from the person's growth and development within, rather than coercion from without.

This theory assumes that the task of the actor on the outside is to help the individual to broaden and form good methods of *perception* on the inside of himself. Good maneuvering tactics may work, but their tenure is usually short.

Academicians claim that this should be the new approach to learning. They say that we should no longer emphasize t*eaching* in our schools, but we should stress *learning*.

The great Carl Rogers once said to a group of teachers that he was no longer interested in the techniques of *teaching*. He said that from that time on he wanted to become a *learner* with other *learners*.

He said that he was convinced that what can be delivered by word-of-mouth from one person to another, is relatively unimportant in influencing behavior. He came to believe that the things that influence behavior are **discovered** internally, gradually, by the receiver.

The question is not how good is the teacher. The question is, is there is any learning taking place, and how has that learning came about. To find the solution to this problem, it is wise to ask what are the basic theories, principles, or axioms that guide one's pursuit?

If learning (not teaching) is the goal for changing behavior, one must ask what are the **determinants** impact or control their perceptions? If we know some of the determinants of perception we will have some tools to use with the student. These tools will enable the student to **discover** the truths that he will need to advance his/her development.

To that end, consider this axiom of perceptual theory:

**The human being
always acts to protect
or enhance what he sees
as his self-image.**

Now, let us move to the practical application of this theory. If people act on how they see things, what causes people to see things that the way they do. Two people do not always see things in the same way. How can you handle that concept? As we have just suggested, you handle it by asking 'what are the factors that influence our perceptions and the way that we see things?'

There are at least six *perceptual determinants*. These *determinants* cause us to perceive the world the way we do. If we need behavioral change, we do not attack the behavior—we attack the factors that cause the perceptions, because behavior comes from our views of what is appropriate.

Change a person's perceptions, and you automatically change his behavior. What are those determinates?

BELIEF
What we believe determines what and how we see the outside world.
Illustration—I believe that Sam doesn't like me and I have believed it for a long time. One day Sam comes up to me and says "Armstrong, you are really a great guy."

How do I see that action? Since I believe that he does not like me, I say to myself, 'I wonder what he is up to? I know he doesn't like me so what is he trying to do to me?'

The next day Sam comes up to me and says "Hey I saw these chocolates at the store and I know how much you like chocolates, so I bought them for you. Here."

Now, do I thank him and appreciate the gift? No, I believe that he is after something from me. It must be bad because he is trying too hard.

No matter what Sam does or says to me, I reject it because I believe that Sam doesn't really like me. My belief will keep me from accepting anything Sam does. I believe he doesn't like me.

If there is ever any possibility of establishing a good relationship between us, Sam is either going to have to change my belief, or I will. If he can change my belief and prove I am wrong he can do just about anything and I will see it as an act of friendship.

This one concept has implications in all areas of life:

If I *believe* that Republicans are selfish rich people and don't care a bit about the little guys, I will never vote for a Republican no matter who the candidate is.

If I *believe* that Baptists only care about getting my money, I will never go to their churches until they change my belief.

If I *believe* that all products from China are of poor quality, I will never buy from Dollar General, even if they are advertising something that I really want. Until my belief is changed, I will keep my dollars in my pocket.

If I *believe* that Northerners are cold, selfish, and snobbish, I will never open up to those Yankees.

If I *believe* that Southerners are country rubes and have no class at all, I will not buy their books, listen to their lecturers, or go to their colleges or universities. Changing the belief systems of these people will not be easy, but until you do, you will not change their behavior.

Behavior is a function of perception and perception is most often the function of beliefs and beliefs often change behavior. The problem is that beliefs are not the only things that influence perceptions.

The behavior of a person may not be the result of some belief—it may have a different factor that determines its behavior. Let's look at another perceptional determinate.

VALUES

Our values often cause us to see things the way we do, and thus influence our behavior. Illustration—Four men go to lunch together and they enjoy a great meal. When the check comes, they split it evenly into four parts and each man puts his amount on the table.

One of the men asks "what about the tip?" Another man, a salesman, says "I'll take care of the tip." Three men walk away from the table—continuing their conversation.

The Salesman lags behind a bit looking through his wallet for the tip. He sees a $50 bill in the wallet, pulls it out and lays it on the table for the waitress.

Now one of the other three men notices the very generous tip. This man is a C.P.A. and when he sees the amount of the tip he says to himself 'That's not right. The tip should only be about $6 or $8 dollars. That's extravagant. He is not careful with his money. I would never hire him in my business.'

Now the salesman said to himself "I sure felt sorry for that waitress. She looked troubled about something. She could be going through a difficult period. It's probably a financial problem. Maybe a good tip will help her get through the day. I've been through hard times and many have helped me when I was down and out. Maybe this extra tip will help her get by."

Now the act of tipping the waitress was seen completely different by the two men, mainly because they each held a different value system. The Salesman's sensitivity and generosity caused him to see the giving of that tip one way. The C.P.A.'s values of frugality and financial customs caused him to see the act as irresponsible.

However, both men could have been wrong. The Salesman could have misread the waitress' behavior as being a financial problem. It could have been only a toothache. The C.P.A. could have been wrong, by putting too much emphasis on the value of money.

To know the determinate of a perception is not easy, but it is more or less permanent. It is hard to discover what makes us see what we do, but if we can discover the determinate, we will have the tool to change behavior.

NEEDS

Another determinant is needs. If one is a Democrat he automatically has the *need* to see nearly everything that a Republican does as a selfish if not an illegal act.

Lawyers **need** to see their clients as innocent victims of someone else's evil or careless deeds.

Mothers **need** to see their children as exceptionally good, talented, or prominent in some way. Perhaps that is why civilization goes on century after century. In all probability those off-spring are banal, common, and uninspiring to all the neighbors. But that does not matter to mother. Mother may be wrong in objective analysis, but she is more than right in providing the care that the children need.

The people we call *teachers* need to see their students as bright, talented, and committed to learning, however that goal is etherial. In all probability, in this day and age someone else will have to provide that support that a child needs.

Writers **need** to see their products as ground-breaking, life-changing, and sourced from a genius mind. Why else would anyone spend—hour after hour—day after day—year after year—scribbling words that few will ever read.

Salesmen **need** to see everyone as potential customers. If they don't have this perception, they will soon be herding cattle in lonely Wyoming.

It is not always possible to know if a behavior is caused by a belief, a value, or need, but until you make that determination you will be unsuccessful in providing an adequate basis for action.

Life is not easy in understanding why we and others act the way we do, but we must hone our own skills of observation and analysis in determining why we and our friends see things the way they do.

ATTITUDES

What is an attitude? We all know that they exist, and we can usually detect a person who has one. But what is it?

My definition is that an attitude is a **belief** that has been held for so long a time, that it is not noticed anymore. It becomes an **attitude** at some time, without our even noticing it and without the person holding it, even knows that he has it.

Just as beliefs may be true or false, so can attitudes. Many strong attitudes are objectively false, but they still exist. Other attitudes can be true and altruistic, but they are only mirrors of what we have long believed.

I lived in South Africa for a time and learned something about attitudes. Seldom was any belief about black citizens expressed openly, but the attitude was always there—apparent and persistent.

At another time, I lived in the South—Atlanta, Georgia to be specific. I was there with my major professor, completing my dissertation for the doctorate in Sociology of Religion.

This was at a time when segregation was the law. The citizens were divided by color and they lived with that status throughout their education.

One day, my professor suggested that I consider enrolling in Atlanta University which was an all-black institution. It was against the law, but with my professor's encouragement I wiggled through the regulations and became the only white student in a university of black students.

It was against the law and none of the black students had ever had a white person in their classes either. All teachers were black and most had never sat in a classroom with white students.

A couple of the professors had gone North to attend university where they were the only black students in a sea of white students. It was a rare experience for learning about prejudice. (I have written a book about that time in Atlanta. The book is available on Amazon and from me directly. The title is WILL IT BE DANGEROUS?)

In contrast my family moved to Alberta, Canada when I was in my early teens. My father was invited to be Dean of a small college and it was his responsibility to admit new students for enrollment.

One day he came home in a real panic. He had just received an enrollment application from a student from Barbados. The word Barbados indicated that the student was a black person. My father, a southerner, panicked at the

24

thought that he would have to assign this black person to room with one of our white students. He knew that this could cause a stir.

As he talked to some of the more mature students he found that it was not a problem. In fact the only problem would be that all of the students would fight for that privilege of living with the new student. Everyone wanted to be his roommate.

In our town of Red Deer, Alberta I found that all black persons were totally welcome, but Indians were not. Being from Oklahoma we were used to Indians being in every phase of community life and this prejudice seemed strange

I remember going out to eat in a restaurant and a big sign at the door shouted, "NO INDIANS ALLOWED." This prejudice against Indians existed in all community life and was unsettling to a young teenager.

Attitudes take a long time to develop, and they take a long time to be changed. And in the meantime behavior continues to be directed by those mysterious attitudes. They are so hard to kill. Wrong or bad perceptions are too often the function of bad attitudes.

SELF EXPERIENCE

Our experiences also determine our behavior. Let me illustrate this truth. Down in a small town in Oklahoma a group of older men have coffee together each morning to gossip and share opinions. It is not an official meeting of any kind. It just happens that several of them have developed the habit of eating breakfast together at Momma's cafe.

The subject matter up for discussion can range from Trump, to the local basketball team. Nothing of local importance ever comes from these times, but a lot of world-problems are solved.

One morning Hiram, who happens to be a county supervisor said "Guys, a fella up from Dallas has been in town a couple of days looking at land. He apparently has a group of Dallas big-shots who want to buy a big parcel of land and divide it and develop it for week-end retreats for families who want to get away from the bustle of big-city life. They want a really big piece of land and price is not too important.

"I know of a thousand acres out pretty close to the lake, that would be ideal for them. We could get it for about a millions dollars, and I think we can sell it to them for two million. We can double our money almost over night, and they are cash customers.

"I have spent two days showing them land and if we can keep the realtors our of the deal, we can make a tidy profit. Any of you guys interested. I'm in for a quarter million right now. All I need is another $750,000. And one of the owners of the land says he would come in for $350,000. Now all we need to make this thing fly is 4 guys to come up with $100,000 each. George, how much you in for?"

"I'll take $100,000 of it, but I want to see your $250,000 in the pot before I write my check."

"Well, I know that Ed at the Bank will be in for $100,000. He told me last week that he was looking for something to do."

"Any of you other guys *in*? Tom?"

"Yeah. I'll take $100,000 if Ed will loan it to me. I'm sure he will. He always does what I ask him to do" Count me in. Ben, you ought to get in on this, too. You got enough money to buy Texas."

"Well I don't have that much money, but I plan to keep what I got. Government bonds don't pay too much, but they are safe. Count me out."

Analysis:

Tom looks at this deal as a sure thing. The last few ventures that he has gone into with Hiram have been winners. Tom sees this as another winner. He would buy almost anything that Hiram floats. Tom has made money on nearly everything that he has invested in and so he sees this as another opportunity for success

Now Ben is a good guy, but the last few investments that he has made, have lost money. He looks at this investment as being risky. He sees it as another opportunity to lose money. He will not invest."

Behavior is a function of perception. Anyone who has seen too many failures will see any new venture as another possibility for failure. And if a man has a string of success, he will probably see that anything that he invests in will make him money. Behavior is a function of perceptions.

The ramification of this one theory is effective in business, marriage, and all sorts of relationships. Success often breeds more success. Failure often breeds more failure. Parents, particularly, should learn this lesson well. The future of their children may well be in the balance.

THREAT OR FEAR
Persons under threat cannot see anything more than the approaching threat. When fear captures a person, the person shuts down, and cannot see or make a rational decision.

A child looks out into the dark and can see all kinds of monsters. An adult looking into the dark may see no monsters at all. The perceptions held inside of us can be the causes of all forms of outside behavior.

Now since there are many determinants of our behavior, before we make any final conclusion we must decide which of these six determinates is the one that is effecting a particular behavior. AND, more importantly is it just one determinate or are there several determinates affecting the behavior?

This rather new perceptual psychology is not an easy answer to behavior, but it offers a better possibility than Stimulus/Response or Behaviorism. More importantly it is a better foundation for facilitating learning than the older methods.

Socrates, the ancient Greek philosopher, thought of himself as a **mid-wife** of ideas. He had as his goal the process of helping young Athenians pull from within themselves truth that was hidden. He emphasized the

discovery of truth that is within the person, rather than the acceptance of truth from an outside source.

One other axiom in perceptual psychology that should be mastered is this:

Any piece of information
will have its effect on the
individual to the degree that
that individual
discovers
personal meaning.

Personal meaning is an important element in affecting behavior. Most of the information relayed to us through TV, teachers, bosses, buddies, etc. will have little effect on our behavior, because the information does not have "personal meaning to us."

For instance a teacher announces to her class that a certain mathematical formula that she is offering must be learned, because if it is not learned the student will never become president of General Motors.

Now this warning will have no effect on the students' behavior because it has no personal meaning to any of them. They are not thinking about becoming the president of any corporation. Indeed, they are only vaguely aware of what a corporation is. NO PERSONAL MEANING HERE. NO DESIRED BEHAVIOR ENSUES.

On the other hand if the teacher had said that in learning that formula it would guarantee that they would get a place on the baseball team—a quick response would have come from many of the students.

<u>Any piece of information will have its effect on human behavior, to the degree that that individual discovers personal meaning.</u>

Think about selling freezers to Aleutians. How would you find much personal meaning?

How would you find personal meaning in selling tanning lamps to nigerians?

You cannot get appropriate behavior from a person without finding personal meaning to that person.

A man on a stroll walks down the street and observes a crowd of people a block ahead of him. Strange. He wonders what the commotion is all about.

Soon he sees a man coming from that direction walking towards him. He stops the man and asks "What's going on down there?"

The man replies that he doesn't know but there was a newspaper reporter taking notes in the middle of the group.

The first man continues on down toward the crowd and meets another man coming from the crowd. He stops the man and asks: "What's going on down there?"

The man replies "Well a lady told me that some neighborhood boy was digging a cave and it collapsed on him, and they are trying to get him out. They don't know how deep he is in."

The man hurries on and sees the newspaper reporter and asks "What's the scoop? Who is that boy?"

The reporter replies that a fireman told him that they think the boy's name is Jerry Burns.

"JERRY BURNS? THAT'S MY SON." and immediately that man runs to the hole, grabs a shovel and franticly starts shoveling as hard as he can.

End of Story.

Now the man's behavior changes gradually in proportion to the information that he receives. Early on, he sees no personal meaning in the crowd. Later he sees that it is a community event and he has a little more interest. Finally, when he learns the name of the boy he finds the greatest of personal meaning and his behavior reflects that intense personal meaning.

This axiom has intense power for behavior.

The politician will offer great public programs for food and health, because she knows that this will provide personal meaning to the poor. She gets elected.

The football coach will tell his team that this year they have a chance to win the State championship and no team ever before in the history of the school has accomplished that fete. Personal meaning!

To those who wish to change negative behavior into positive behavior, they must first find out what gives the person, personal meaning. The manipulation of people towards a desirable goal can be mostly ineffectual.

Helping others to grow their perceptions and develop their maturity will bring out behavior that cannot be procured any other way. At nearly every point of action, a person elects to do that which seems to hold the greatest promise for maintaining or enhancing his self well-being. Think about it.

There is one final consideration in determining one's personal perceptions. I call this the *moral compass*. Although, this may be vaguely seen as some nebulous something floating around an issue, it is usually not well defined.

My father was a preacher, and was definitely concerned about **moral** behavior. He felt that moral behavior was much more than ethical behavior—he married the concept with belief, truth, values and nearly everything else that was a part of the person's existence.

Early in my life he stressed that I should develop a moral compass that would determine not only my behavior, but also my internal and contemplative life. He agreed with the adage that "as a man thinketh, so *is* he." What a person thinks about will shape the other determinates of behavior.

Since my father chose philosophy as his major in college, I decided to follow his example. I entered the murky waters of contemplative thought, and began my search for a reliable moral compass.

It was not long until I discovered a sentence that I adopted as my moral compass. I began earnestly to follow it as a guide for my own behavior. Years later, I found myself as a father of a great teenaged daughter. For some reason she wanted to give me a gift—a gift of real personal meaning.

She surprised me with a beautiful piece of needlework that she had cross stitched herself. It was a beautifully designed verse—my moral compass.

I, of course, had it framed and today several decades later it hangs in the most prominent place in my study. It is still the best guide that I know—a true and reliable moral compass.

Finally brethren,
whatsoever things are true,
whatsoever things are honest,
whatsoever things are just,
whatsoever things are pure,
whatsoever things are lovely.
whatsoever things are of good report,
if there be any virtue,
if there be any praise,
Think on these things.
Philippians 4:8

Companion Books in the
Win With Wisdom Series

"WISE Methods for WISE people"
Take Ten Steps to Reach Your Goals

Nearly everyone knows WHAT the goals are or WHAT they want. Few people know HOW to get the WHAT. A new movement has been formed to help people capture the skill of HOW to get things done, or as they call it how to **GTD**. This book is a primer or beginners guide. It is a road map which anyone can read or follow. It involves moving from a beginning point to a second point and then through eight other points which will help nearly anyone to GTD or arrive at a desirable destination.

Any reader who will invest 30 minutes of their time and $5) will be rewarded with a tool worth thousands of dollars and hours of new time.

"Save Yourselves with WISDOM"
How to avoid the Dangers of Tomorrow

Tomorrow will bring a cup of promise and a vat of dangers. No one will be exempt from either. The only solution is too get to know both and plan to avoid the dangers and profit from the promises.

Central to the book is a letter written by a wealthy tycoon to his wealthy clients. What he writes is appropriate   for the rich, and important for average families as well. To ignore his warnings would be sheer folly.

This book faces the warnings head-on and points to practical solutions. An investment of only 30 minutes of your time could be the best investment that you will make this year. The tycoons letter is a must-read.

"It's WISE To Know The Big Picture"
The strategies of *Getting by Giving*

This book is based on a story told by a very wealthy investor to an educator seeking a large financial gift. The educator received NO MONEY, but he was given a valuable secret that would always bring wealth to anyone brave enough to use it.

The book is small and only costs $5.00 and 30 minutes of your time, but you and the ones that you care about should have it. It could change your future.

"The WISDOM of Knowing yourself
and others"
Why you and others do what they do

Psychology has become one of the most popular studies in colleges and universities. Unfortunately it has been seized by the academicians who have morphed it into a complex tool, available only to the esoteric.

This book molds psychology into a useful every-day tool for average persons. There are no long words or complex formulas. The average person can use what he reads to understand himself and whose with whom he lives and works.

That it is a commonsense book for daily living is its merit. Don't show it to your professor, analyst or therapist. Read it yourself and use it daily.

"WISDOM on Fire"
It takes more than one stick to burn BIG

This small book is big on emotion, concepts and inspiration. It can be read in less than half an hour, but it should be read only a few pages at a time.

And even if your memory is fading you will remember many phrases, sentences and passages for years to come. This book will be a unique experience. Don't miss it.

These books are all available from Amazon.com.

Go to Amazon, and on Amazons search type: Kenneth Shelby Armstrong Books. Select the book that you want and pay Amazon.

To contact the author.

Kenneth Shelby Armstrong Th.D., Ed.D.

Email: KennethWrites@me.com

Phone: 1-580-873-2377

Address: 1036 Holiday Acres Drive

Fort Towson, OK 74735

Now, take a few minutes
and look at some of the other books
that Dr. Armstrong has written.

Whatever Happened To Robin?

Kenneth Shelby Armstrong
Publisher: Create Space
Available: Amazon or
Direct from Author
347 Pages
Copyright 2015

On the shores of Lake Biwa near Kyoto, Japan, a distinguished American bishop laid his head in the lap of a lovely Japanese woman and died. His death opened a secret that he had held since he was a young G.I. exploring the ruins of Hiroshima and Nagasaki with a young Japanese girl friend. The explosion of the secret shook a prominent American family and its church.

When he left Japan he promised to return and marry the girl of his dreams, but circumstances caused him to break that promise. Nevertheless, each New Year's Day he wrote her letters reaffirming his love and promising to return to her.

For decades he served his church as Bishop, but he never gave up his pledge to return to Robin. Nearing death he could delay no longer so he, used what strength he had to return to Japan and he laid his head in the lap of a lovely woman and died. But, to know the real secret you must read Whatever Happened to Robin?.

Will It Be Dangerous? Could I Get Killed?

Kenneth Shelby Armstrong
Publisher: Create Space
Available: Amazon or
Direct from Author
129 Pages
Copyright 2015

"No! No! No You're looking at this thing all wrong. This will be a great educational experience. Just think of it! It's 1953 and segregation is the law of the State of Georgia and most other States in the South. A white graduate student walks into an all-negro University, say Atlanta University, and tries to enroll. What do you think would happen? This could be a life-changing experience for you, and it could bring about real change."

"That's what I'm thinking about. This life-changing experiment could get me killed. Have you ever heard of the Ku Klux Klan? If they hear about this I will be dead meat. If by some miracle the university should let me in, they will be breaking the law. It's illegal for them to accept a white student. I could even go to jail. I could get killed. And what if your Dean heard that you were advising one of your students to break the law? It could get you fired. But why should I worry? I'll be dead." The story of the book is, that I did get enrolled and I'm still alive and significantly more educated.

How To Strive, Thrive, And Stay Alive in Prison

Kenneth Shelby Armstrong
Publisher: Create Space
Available: Amazon or
Direct from Author
117 Pages
Copyright 2015

More than a million prisoners are now behind bars; eating three bland meals a day with never a change; each night they are serenaded by a chorus of snores from which there is no escape; they spend time in planning revenge on some member of their families or some policeman or judge who did them wrong; they wait for that special letter that never comes. Too often mail call is a downer. It's a tough life for the men, but much harder on the women.

Broken dreams become nightmares. Soft memories are crushed by harsh treatment from detention officials. Visiting hours are too brief and saying goodbye to family and small children erupts in tears that will continue for hours.

But some in prison find forgiveness and others discover that there is hope. Some discover beauty in unexpected places. Faith, hope, and love, live there too.

My Very Best Stories

Kenneth Shelby Armstrong
Publisher: Create Space
Available: Amazon or
Direct from Author
138 Pages
Copyright 2015

There is a really great editor/owner of the newspaper in the town where I live. He knows everybody and everybody knows him. In these days there are few towns and newspapers like the one we have in Hugo, Oklahoma. I read his editorials every day and hidden inside of each one is pungent information, sparkling humor, and honest concern for the town where he has lived all of his life, and which many of us have adopted.

Against all odds he has kept our newspaper something that we look forward to getting. One day he asked me to let him publish some of my short stories in the paper. I gladly accepted the assignment. It was so well received that we decided to publish those stories in a book. It's now available and the range of interest is broad enough to capture the interest of people even though they live in New York City or Los Angeles. These are stories for everyone.

I Was A Reluctant Guest
Kenneth Shelby Armstrong
Publisher: Create Space
Available: Amazon or
Direct from Author
236 Pages
Copyright 2015

Being in prison can be an
exciting adventure. Every inmate has some great story to
tell–and that over and over again. But the stories that come
from prison are rooted in a minutia of facts, most of which
are boring and void of meaning. The facts of each
prisoner's case may be interesting only to a weird attorney
or some other prisoner who is looking for some way to get
out. What do you do when you are looking at twenty years
in each dreadful place?

O f
more interest than facts are the emotions and feelings alive
in each prison. For the most part the emotions are kept
within specifically prescribed boundaries, but too often
they spill out like volcanic ash. The results can be fights,
riots, and escapes. Neither guards nor reluctant guests look
forward to such events. But you will begin to understand
the drama of prison, inside and out.

He Died A Hero

Kenneth Shelby Armstrong
Publisher: Create Space
Available: Amazon or
Direct from Author
211 Pages
Copyright 2015

I n our current culture a hero is someone, dressed in a cape and flying through the air with the greatest of ease to release some damsel who has gotten into the clutches of an ogre with warts. Of course the drama takes place on some remote planet located just above Kansas City. The plot is compelling and people will pay $15 just to experience the unreality of some weirdo's imagination.

O n the other hand an unadorned reality is a country boy wearing patched overalls and sporting a straw hat with holes in the brim and a black sweat band earned while picking cotton under an Oklahoma sun, to earn a few cents to put bread on the table during the peak of the Great Depression. After supper he will study until his eye lids shut his brain down, but he is committed to getting a college education–the first in his family. With the diploma placed in the back pocket of his overalls he marched out to serve his God and those in need. What a Story!

The two most
important days in
your life are the day
you are born and the
day you find out why.

-Mark Twain

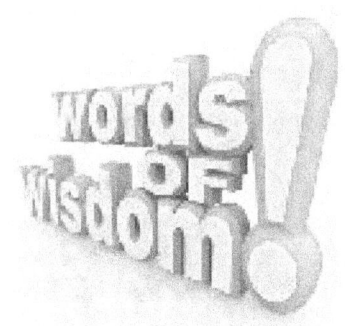

www.ingramcontent.com/pod-product-compliance
Lightning Source LLC
Chambersburg PA
CBHW071134280526
45787CB00003B/1276